Your Body

Eating

Anna Sandeman

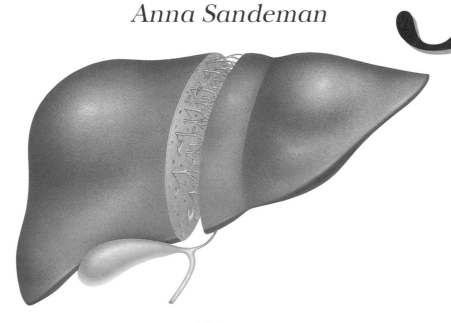

W
FRANKLIN WATTS
LONDON • SYDNEY

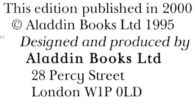

This edition published in 2000
© Aladdin Books Ltd 1995
Designed and produced by
Aladdin Books Ltd
28 Percy Street
London W1P 0LD

First published in
Great Britain in 1995 by
Franklin Watts
96 Leonard Street
London EC2A 4XD

Design: David West Children's Books
Designer: Edward Simkins
Illustrator: Ian Thompson
Editor: Liz White
Picture Research: Brooks Krikler
Research
Consultants: Dr R Levene MB.BS,
DCH, DRCOG
Jan Bastoncino Dip. Ed., teacher of
biology and science to 5-12 year-olds

ISBN 0-7496-1975-9 (hardback)
ISBN 0-7496-3900-8 (paperback)

Printed in Belgium

A CIP catalogue record for this book is
available from the British Library.

Photocredits
Abbreviations: t-top, m-middle, b-bottom,
r-right, l-left
All the photos in this book are by Roger Vlitos
except: 6t, 7t, 8-9b, 13b, 23tr, 23mr & 28-29t
Frank Spooner Pictures; 22r & 23br Paul
Nightingale; 23l Eye Ubiquitous; 28m Associated
British Pictures Co. (Courtesy Kobal Collection.)

Contents

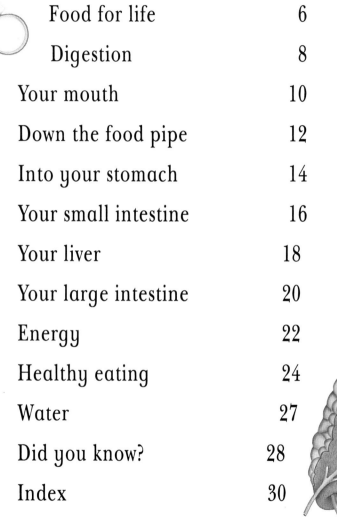

Food for life

All animals must eat to stay alive. Food is needed for energy and for growth. Food also helps to mend parts of the body which have been hurt, or have gone wrong.

The kind of food each animal eats depends on where it lives, its size, shape and strength. Monkeys will eat almost anything they can find. Penguins dive for fish in the icy Antarctic sea. They swallow a fish in a single gulp. Lions chase zebra across the hot African plains.

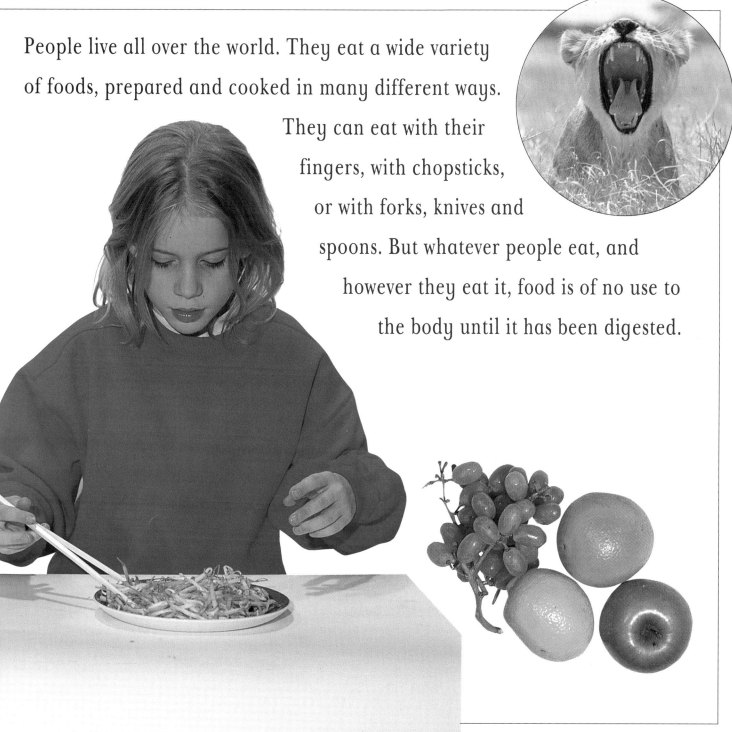

People live all over the world. They eat a wide variety of foods, prepared and cooked in many different ways. They can eat with their fingers, with chopsticks, or with forks, knives and spoons. But whatever people eat, and however they eat it, food is of no use to the body until it has been digested.

Digestion

Digestion starts as soon as you put food in your mouth. It carries on for about 18 hours as the food travels through your digestive system. This is a series of tunnels and caves inside your body. These are all different sizes, shapes and lengths.

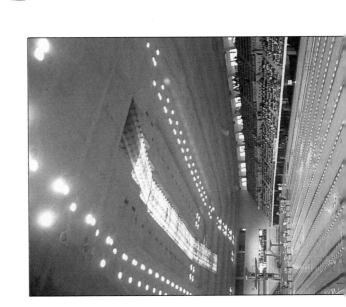

Oesophagus

Stomach

Large intestine

Small intestine

If they were laid in a straight line, they would stretch over eight metres – the width of an average swimming pool!

Your body digests food slowly by breaking it down into smaller and smaller pieces, separating it into useful parts – nutrients and waste matter. Food is completely digested when it has passed from your digestive system into your blood. Your blood then carries the nutrients around your body.

Food is broken down in the digestive system.

Nutrients pass from the digestive system into the blood.

Your mouth

Each part of your mouth has a special job to do. If you eat an apple, you bite into it with your front teeth. The four teeth in the middle of your top and bottom jaws, your incisors, are used for cutting and chopping. The sharp, fang-like teeth either side of your incisors are used for cutting and tearing. These are your canine teeth.

Your tongue pushes the apple back to your molars for chewing.

Incisor   Canine   Molar

You have molars in both your upper and lower jaws. Your molars are wider than your front teeth and have bumpy tops. Run a finger along the edges of your upper teeth and feel the difference.

Your molars grind the apple until it becomes a lumpy mash. Your tongue rolls the mash into a ball.

Saliva in your mouth makes chewing easier, it also helps you to taste. Sometimes just thinking about your favourite food will make your mouth fill with saliva. Try it and see.

Down the food pipe

Your tongue pushes the ball of mash into your food pipe. This is called your oesophagus. As you swallow, a flap (your epiglottis) drops over your windpipe. This stops food going down the wrong way.

Sometimes your epiglottis does not drop down in time. When this happens, you have to cough hard until the food is blown out of your windpipe.

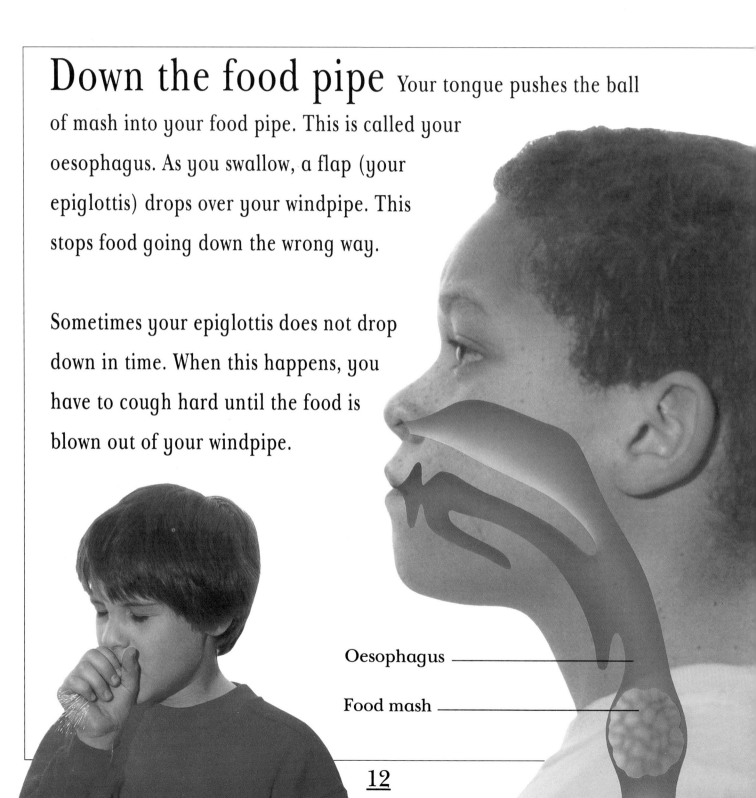

Oesophagus

Food mash

Your oesophagus is a stretchy tube about 25 centimetres long. Its walls are made of muscles which squeeze food downwards. They do this without you thinking about it. To see how they work, put a tennis ball down a long sock. Like the muscles in your oesophagus, you have to squeeze your hands hard together just behind the ball to move it along.

Muscles squeeze behind the food to push it down.

Because food is squeezed along your oesophagus, and does not simply fall down it, it is possible to eat in almost any position – even standing on your head! This means that astronauts can enjoy a meal even when floating around their cabin! (But remember it is safest to eat when you are upright.)

Into your stomach

At the bottom of your oesophagus, the mash passes into your stomach. This is a stretchy bag shaped like a boxing glove. It lies just below your ribs. Food stays here for two to three hours.

During this time, your stomach churns the mash with gastric juices from your stomach wall. These juices kill any germs in the mash and help to break the food down into smaller parts. When the mash has turned into a kind of thick soup, it is ready to leave your stomach.

Rib cage

Stomach

Soup food

Gate of muscle

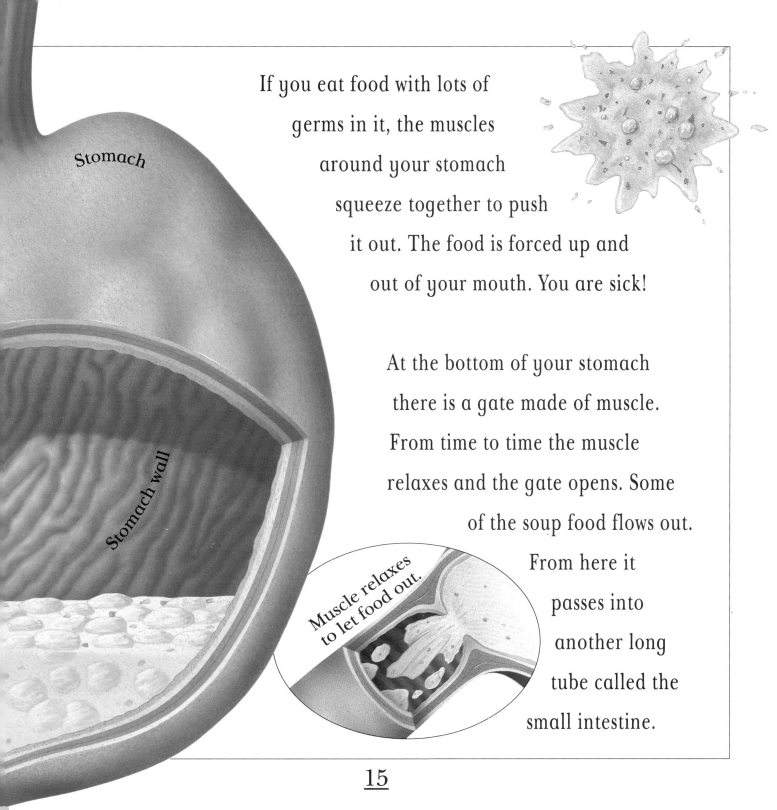

Stomach

Stomach wall

Muscle relaxes to let food out.

If you eat food with lots of germs in it, the muscles around your stomach squeeze together to push it out. The food is forced up and out of your mouth. You are sick!

At the bottom of your stomach there is a gate made of muscle. From time to time the muscle relaxes and the gate opens. Some of the soup food flows out. From here it passes into another long tube called the small intestine.

Your small intestine
Your small intestine is about seven metres long. That's as long as five seven year-olds laid head to toe! It can take up to ten hours for the soup food to travel from one end to the other.

In the first part of the small intestine the soup food is mixed with juices from your pancreas and bile from your liver which helps to break it down even further.

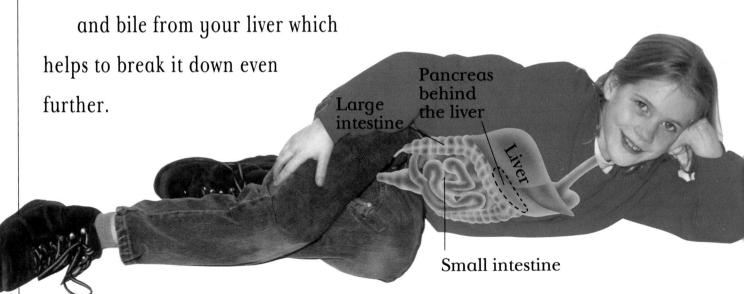

Large intestine

Pancreas behind the liver

Liver

Small intestine

It is then squeezed on through your intestine becoming more and more watery as it goes.

As the almost liquid food reaches the end of your small intestine, nutrients pass through its walls into your blood. The walls are lined with thousands of tiny fingers, called villi, to help digest the nutrients more quickly.

Your blood carries most of the nutrients to your liver. Undigested food travels on to your large intestine.

Villi

Blood vessels

Blood vessels absorb the nutrients.

Your liver

Your liver lies mostly on your right side, protected by your lower ribs. It weighs between one and two kilogrammes. That's about the same weight as your brain.

Before any food can be used by your body, it has to be cleaned and prepared by your liver. Your liver sieves through the nutrients and blood to take out any leftover waste. It turns some of the waste into bile which travels through the bile ducts and out of the liver.

Liver

Gall bladder

Liver

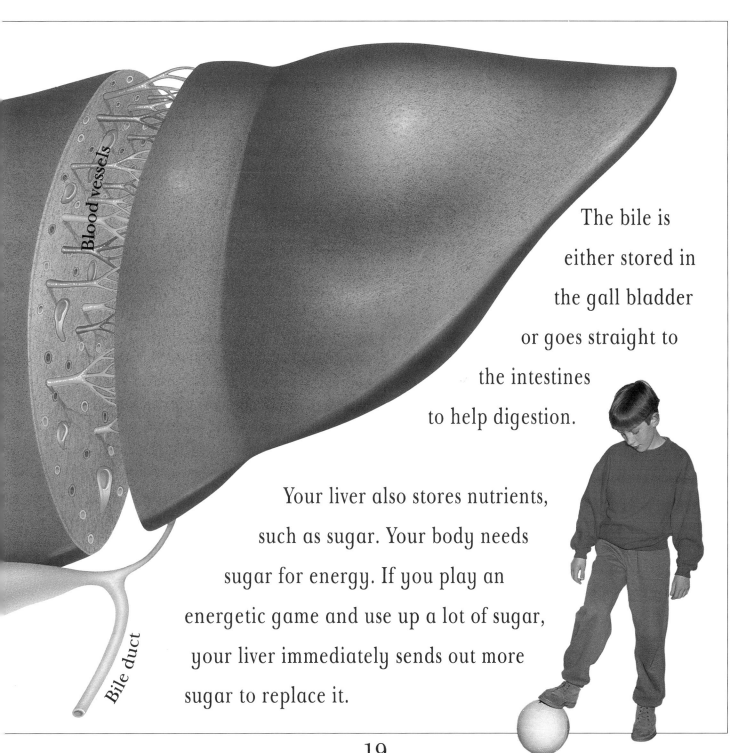

Blood vessels

Bile duct

The bile is
either stored in
the gall bladder
or goes straight to
the intestines
to help digestion.

Your liver also stores nutrients,
such as sugar. Your body needs
sugar for energy. If you play an
energetic game and use up a lot of sugar,
your liver immediately sends out more
sugar to replace it.

Your large intestine

Your large intestine carries undigested food and water from your small intestine up, across and down to your rectum.

Your large intestine is wider than your small intestine, but only half as long. It takes up to 24 hours for its contents to complete the journey from beginning to end.

As food and water travel along, a lot of water is sucked through the wall of your large intestine into your blood. Then only waste food is left. Slowly it gets harder. By the time it reaches your rectum, it is quite solid. This solid waste, called faeces, is stored in your rectum until you are ready to push it out through your anus when you go to the lavatory.

Oesophagus

Liver

Stomach

Large intestine

Small intestine

Rectum

Energy

Most of the food you eat is turned into energy. Some people need more energy – and more food – than others. Babies and young children need less food than grown-ups. As you grow into your teens you need more.

By the time you reach your mid-teens, you will probably eat as much as your parents. Tall, well-built people need more food than shorter, thinner people. Men usually need more than women. If you eat more food than you need it is stored as fat inside your body.

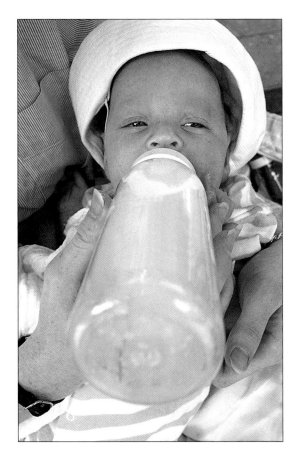

You use energy all the time. Even when you are asleep, your body is using energy to keep warm and make your heart beat. The more active you are, the more energy you use. Which of the activities shown in these pictures do you think uses up most energy? Which uses the least? Put them in order. The answers are at the bottom of the page. Look in a mirror to see if you are right.

Swimming uses the most energy followed by cycling. Watching television uses the least.

Swimming

Watching television

Cycling

Healthy eating

Nutrients are found in food. There are five main types; proteins, carbohydrates, fats, vitamins and mineral salts.

Nutrients are absorbed from the food you eat and used by your body. To stay healthy you should eat the right amount of each type of nutrient every day. Each has one or more special jobs to do in your body.

Proteins help you to grow strong and healthy. The body cannot store them so it is important to eat some food containing proteins every day. They are found in eggs, milk, cheese, fish, meat, beans and nuts.

Bread

Potatoes

Nuts

Meat

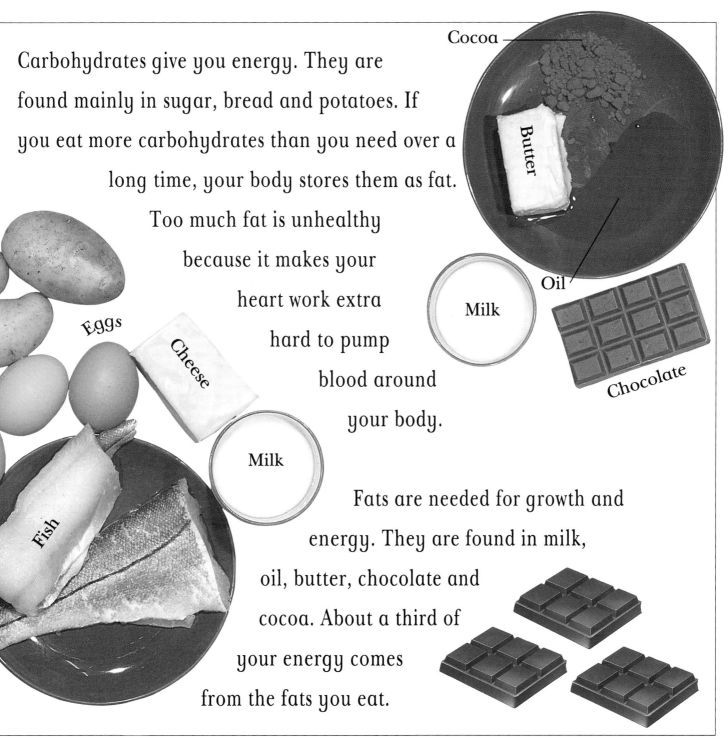

Carbohydrates give you energy. They are found mainly in sugar, bread and potatoes. If you eat more carbohydrates than you need over a long time, your body stores them as fat. Too much fat is unhealthy because it makes your heart work extra hard to pump blood around your body.

Cocoa

Butter

Oil

Milk

Chocolate

Eggs

Cheese

Milk

Fish

Fats are needed for growth and energy. They are found in milk, oil, butter, chocolate and cocoa. About a third of your energy comes from the fats you eat.

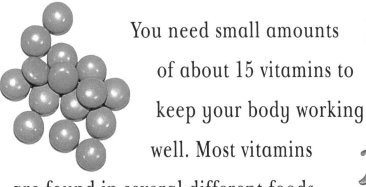

You need small amounts of about 15 vitamins to keep your body working well. Most vitamins are found in several different foods. Vitamin C is present only in fresh fruit and vegetables – especially oranges. Vitamin C is important for healthy skin and bones. It also helps wounds to heal.

Mineral salts are needed only in small amounts. Calcium, in milk and cheese, helps to build healthy bones. Iodine, in fish, is important for growth.

Water

You should drink plenty of water every day. You lose up to two and a quarter litres of water each day when you breathe out, sweat and go to the lavatory. You replace the water by eating as well as drinking. Half of all food is made up of water.

Ask your friends what they like to eat. Make a chart to show everyone's favourite food. Which food do people like the best? Now plan a healthy lunch. Compare it with your favourite meal. Which is better for you?

Foods

Beans

Hamburger

Apple

Cheese

Pasta

Chocolate

Fish

Eggs

Number of people

Did you know? ... that by the age of 70 you will have eaten more than 30,000 kilogrammes of food? That's the same as six elephants or two blue whales.

... that although you could live for up to three weeks without food, you would die in just three days without water?

... that your body has as much calcium as 340 sticks of chalk?

... that nearly three-quarters of your body is made up of water?

... that the human stomach can hold up to one and a half litres of food and water?

Compare this with a large dog – almost three litres; a pig – between six and nine litres; a horse – between ten and 20 litres; a cow – about 150 litres.

... that every day you produce about one and three-quarter litres of saliva?

Index